My Awkward Adolescence

Jeff Ryan

Broken Lamp Publishers

Nashville

Broken Lamp Publishers

Nashville, TN

First edition published 2015.

Designed by Jeff Ryan

Ryan, Jeff.
My Awkward Adolescence/ by Jeff Ryan

ISBN-13: 978-0692594490 (pbk)
ISBN-10: 0692594493 (pbk)

To Dj

I promised that people would remember your name

Also by Jeff Ryan

For more information visit
www.jeffryanwriting.wordpress.com/books

To Leave or Die in Nashville
A Broken Lamp Publishers Book

"To Leave Or Die in Nashville... will make you laugh and
will have you wishing you were young again."
-Jaime McAlistar

"Jeff Ryan showcases a poetic voice very comfortable with
its humor... [To Leave or Die in Nashville] is deserving of
great recognition."
-Caroline Saunders

Chain Letters and Other Poems
Amazon Best-Seller

"I think what sets this book apart is Ryan's stronger
imagery and subversive sense of humor. Several of the
pieces... struck my brain with just the right tone, and
resonated for longer than I'd expected them to."
-Charles Haynes

"[Ryan]... shows shine and promise from the beginning."
-Samantha Ripley

Contents

Prologue

Introduction   3

Confessional   8

Welcome to These Days, They Are Pretty Much the Same

Time   13

BW   14

I've Always   15

July   18

Yeah haha   19

Sjo   20

The Red Door Saloon   21

To My Back-Home Boston Girl   22

Sext II   25

Lonnie's   26

Aysa   27

One Day You Look Up And See The Sun Eclipsed By A Cloud of Crows   28

Allardt, TN   29

You   32

Natchez Trace   33

The Lonely Bones of Winter

Love Poem   37

To the Ex-Girlfriend and Her Next Boyfriend   39

11   43

Movies   44

AC   45

Snow   46

Interstellar   47

Missing Out   50

The Part About Ghosts

Homecoming 53
KS 55
Naubuc 57
Waiting for God 58
Elle 59
Boys 66
Trigonometry 68
Homeroom at GHS 69
October 71
Elle, A Memory 74
Scars 77
Une Fin 79
February 82
Time Passed 84
Dear Elle 95
A Poem for my 20th Birthday 98

Epilogue

Motivation 103

My Awkward Adolescence

"It is an act too often neglected," said the fox. It means to establish ties."

"'To establish ties'?"

"Just that," said the fox. "To me, you are still nothing more than a little boy who is just like a hundred thousand other little boys. And I have no need of you. And you, on your part, have no need of me. To you, I am nothing more than a fox like a hundred thousand other foxes. But if you tame me, then we shall need each other. To me, you will be unique in all the world. To you, I shall be unique in all the world . . ."

-Antoine de Saint-Exupéry

Prologue

This is the third book I have written.

I'm telling myself that it is okay to keep writing books. Like this is something totally sustainable that I can do with my life, you know? And like eating peanut butter and jelly eight times a week in between working shifts at a TexMex restaurant and sleeping on a couch in my friend's apartment is just part of the whole "writing process." And some day I can be a writer. Like that can be a real thing.

Maybe it's not a reality but I'm going to try.

Thank you for reading my book.

It makes me really happy that you are here reading the words that I am writing.

Prologues are boring, they say. Just a bunch of long-winded nonsense where the author thanks everyone he's ever met and everyone who would be mad if they didn't get their name thrown in somewhere. Nobody reads prologues any more. Except for you. You're different, and I like that. You get a book, and you go through every page as if between the paper and the ink lie the keys to Atlantis. As if every last word is a piece to a puzzle. So here, tucked inside this prologue, it's all basically a special poem just for you.

My name is Jeff Ryan and this is almost an autobiography. I say almost because autobiographies are for people who have done Important Stuff to tell the Truth about themselves, and to be honest I haven't really done anything important. But this book is True. Some of it happened and some of it didn't, but all of it is True.

I go to Vanderbilt University in Nashville and I major in French which is kind of like saying I am majoring in being unemployed when I graduate. I major in French because when I was seventeen I went to France and kissed a couple of really beautiful girls and I have this problem that when I kiss someone I suddenly think that they are the best thing since sliced bread. Except of all the girls I kissed in France I mostly kissed Jeanne who could make me laugh in four different languages and a smile like she wasn't sure if she should be smiling or not. I called her "chérie" and told her that she was "la plus belle dame du monde" but I said it all with a bad French accent because it was a long time ago and I wasn't very good at French. Then she would call me "cowboy" and "bg" and "bête" but with a very good French accent.

I wanted to kiss her a bunch of times and maybe pack her onto the plane with me so she could be my friend in America too. Except she didn't fit in my suitcase so instead I gave her one of my Vanderbilt t-shirts. Then I left for the US and told her I'd write her a letter every now and then. I wrote her one and then got annoyed by how expensive international post is and then one thing led to another and all things fell apart. Anyways, that's the story of how I accidentally fell for a naive French girl who lived on the beach. That's also the story of why I became a French major. But I already can't even look adults in the eyes when they ask me what my major is and when I do manage to tell them I certainly don't mention Jeanne and I certainly don't mention it's "compliqué" with another "homme" and doesn't even return my facebook messages any more when I'm bored and lonely at 3AM and so why the fuck am I even a French major anyways. Instead I say "I want to get into international business" which is a giant load of bullshit because if I ever have to work in business I'll shoot myself probably.

What I want to do more than everything in the world is write stories. Back in kindergarten I had a teacher named Ms. Rickard and she told us all that we were young authors. And that authors were special. That authors could change the world if they wrote hard enough. Then she gave us all our very own blank books and told us to write a story and fill up the pages and all the girls started writing stories about princesses and kittens while all the boys started writing stories about cars and baseball players. I didn't really like any of that. I named my book "The Book About Everything" because I didn't want to just write one story.

But I filled my book.

I wrote about the smelly monsters who disappeared because they were mean to each other and about a blob of slime who got in a fight with a robot and about a butterfly who was looking for a friend in a thinly-veiled parallel to Homer's Iliad or something like that. It was pretty cerebral in a "I-still-stick-crayons-up-my-nostrils-and-pretend-I'm-a-walrus-to-try-to-get-girls-to-notice-me" kind of way. Now I'm here 15 years later and this is my book about everything again.

Confessional

Writing is two things. Writing is narcissism mostly. It's the vain, naive idea that what you have to say is actually important. It's like trying to move a beach into a parking lot but the only tool you have is a pair of tweezers. It's screaming at the top of your lungs until your throat is raw, only you're stuck in a room with a million other people who are also screaming at the top of their lungs hoping what they have to say is important too.

Writing is also confessional. That's what they mean when they say "write what you know" all the time. You're supposed to confess something and make the typewriter bleed, at least a little bit.

Confession: I think a full moon is probably the prettiest thing in the world. Especially in that early part of the night during autumn when the trees reach out like the hands of skeletons and the air bites your cheeks from the cold and the clouds are black and keep floating across the sky and even though you know werewolves aren't real you keep looking over your shoulder just in case you're being followed.

Confession: I have a crush on a girl who can write like no one I have ever read before and talking to her makes my head feel foggy and when we snapchat I think she is really a beautiful person, aesthetically speaking. I like being a human with her. Unfortunately having a crush on a girl is pretty much my permanent state of being so all my friends tend to just roll their eyes when I tell them that she's different because I really like her and would totally take her on dates and write poems about the way she tilts her head when she smiles. It's like beyond a hopeless romantic and moving more towards a character flaw. A definition of my personal reality style-of-thing.

Confession: I write a lot about girls.

Confession: I wanna write a book one day exclusively out of image macros and not mention girls a single time but idk if that's a good idea since I want people to take me seriously as a writer.

Confession: I think I'm failing out of college. I think it is stressful and pointless and I don't wanna just suck it up and pretend spending 60-75% of my time doing something I hate is an OK way to spend my existence. I only go because I like my friends and the real word is scary and growing up all the way is a sucky thing and everyone tells you your whole life that you have to go to college and if you don't you will be hungry and homeless and die under an overpass out in Houston on a particularly hot and dry August afternoon, which does not sound like a way I want to be spending my August afternoons.

Confession: A few months after I wrote that, I did fail out of college. It ended up being not as terrible as I thought. But I'm back now and I'm trying it out again.

Confession: I sort of lied earlier. This isn't a book about girls or almost an autobiography like I said it was, even though it might seem that way at times. Really it's a book about ghosts.

I'm sorry for putting my ghosts into your life.

Welcome to These Days,
They Are Pretty Much the Same

Time

I could ride with Genghis Khan
On horseback across the known world
For all the time I have killed.
Wasted hours
Weeks
Staring at clocks
Ignoring teachers
Thumbing old photographs.

Counting minutes
Counting anything
Waiting for something to happen.

Is this all there is?

BW

There are a lot of words going on.

The car is moving too fast.

You are playing country music on the radio.
I never liked country music, but for you I always tried to
pretend at
least a little.

Fuck, I say a bunch of times.

Fuck.

You drop me off at my house.
I try not to slam the car door
but
       I do anyways.

It's an accident.

I've Always
> wanted to write a poem about vicodin.

Because in the 10th grade, my leg snapped
Twisted at the knee cap and torn
At my labrum.
> I had to look up the word
"Labrum" in the dictionary in between
Popping pain killers for Breakfast,
Lunch, and Dinner.

I'm not bitter. That's just my luck.
See, when I was born, I was ass-first
Backwards in the womb, with my
Umbilical cord wrapped around my neck
Ready to choke me on the way out.

I feel like that was pretty representative
For how the rest of my life has panned out.

Running away from places and
Meeting new people but forgetting old faces
And always trying to keep up with my currencies
While every new city passes by perfectly
In that I'm never there for very long.

There's a guy up my street
Who says he sells happiness
And offers me some bottles
Tells me "lonely"
> makes shitty ambiance

I don't claim I'm above the influence
So five times a week I try it
But you don't have to finish college to know
It's not happiness if you buy it.

I'm not proud.
> Most days
Are spent alone in my apartment

(With walls that echo from all the space
I live without you) getting
Stoned on cheap weed, listening to
Lana Del Rey and waiting for
The next.

I don't have any kind of exit plan.
No grand ideas for a great escape
But I'm starting to wonder
How much more of this city I can take.

But it's not this city, I know.
That's just an excuse I use
Because I see your stupid fucking Ford
Driving down every fucking street.

I need a change of pace-
An about-face to my warped perspective
Because here I am bitching about how
My ex-girlfriend won't drop the
"Ex" part of her relationship with me

While across the sea they're
Chopping heads off of journalists
And lighting cities on fire
While I sling burritos and margaritas
To tourists on Broadway.

I'm only bitching because it
Brings in the Benjamin's.
After all, even in all the slaughter
You can still find some laughter
If you make it through the blues.

My friend is hosting a costume party
At a house down the street that will
Keep rolling all night.

I'm sorry, though.
I think I forgot the

Vicodin.

July

July like a car crash-
An automobile out of control
At 80-miles-per-hour colliding with
Concrete and steel dividers
Shattering on impact in a flurry
Of glass and crunching metal.

Today the heat is instantaneous.
Dry and suffocating like a wool blanket
Oppressing every inch of flesh.
Maybe I will stop and grab a taco
From my friend Alvaro on 19th
Or get drunk with Aaron in Midtown
With endless whiskey that could double as
Rat poison.

Maybe I will sit alone with my thoughts
And let memories flood back into my head -
Of waking up next to you
Sunlight seeming like it flowed from your body
And the way your eyes fluttered open
To the world-
Letting my hurt play out on my own
Private stage, taking pride in the way it
Bleeds.

Every year they expect that I will fall
Without them. That they will find me
Alone, slack-jawed in a dark room
Eyes faded like the petals
Of flowers caught in July sun.

Yet each year (despite some new bullshit)
My Spartan soul (my donkey soul) survives.

Yeah haha you can touch me.
Yeah haha I'm free next Thursday.
Yeah haha I love Ocean Avenue.
Yeah haha plz touch me.

Sjo

July nights on playground swings
Fireflies with broken wings
As the country sumer sun would set
Our faces eclipsed in silhouette
      We fell in love in summer air

Holding hands through tallest grass
Ignoring hours as they passed
Until our fingers rearranged
The taste of air now something strange

On the night before you left
I cleaned the sheets that we had messed
The reverberation of your laugh compressed
Inside the fireflies of my chest
      I loved you best, I loved you most
      Within my heart, my summer ghost

The Red Door Saloon

I kept looking for love like it was underneath someone else's
Winter hat in the communal lost and found
But instead all I found were orgasms.

Beneath the floor of the Red Door Saloon
Lie two skeletons, wrapped in each other's embrace.
I found them once, blurred by rum and coke.

They are made of plastic.
Everyone knows when you're unstable,
You can't find love in
Stable places.

To My Back-Home Boston Girl

When you told me,
       Choking through your rage
       Your tears
       Your violation

When you told me
What had happened
Was the precise moment
My world tilted off its
Axis
The room
       gyrating
Field of vision shifting
Focus

A
loss
for
Words.

We sat on the phone line,
The static of silence crackling
Between us, keeping us connected across
1,000 miles via satellite.

I would have given everything
To have been in that room with you.
To put my arm around you and
Try to help you hold up your world.
To donate all the strength I had and
All the strength I could borrow
From Atlas and from Samson and
Do it all for you.
All to make your life
A little brighter and make your
Breath a little lighter.

What good were any
Books if I couldn't write you some
Way out of this. If my words were
Useless because I had none for you then.

I say I would have given everything,
What I truly mean is everything.
Because if I'd been close enough to you
To touch, it would mean I were
Close enough to find him,
The man who forced himself on you
Close enough to beat him
Bleed him
Make him suffer for every agony he caused
Every moment you woke up, winded from
Some remembered terror, make him regret the
Moment he ever laid a finger on you
For that I'd give up my world.

Stop
      You said.

Don't feed hate with hate
Don't make this about him or you.
Just write me a poem
One to make me happy.

So I sat
And I wrote.

Wrote you a poem where our fear
Fought against the friction-
Of courage despite all opposition
A poem where we were the winners
The heavy-weight champions of the world
Bloodied and battered but
Victorious, hearts beating against
Olympic medals of bravery and courage.

For the days when we'd tag along together at recess.
Or the time in sixth grade
I wrote a book about a boy and his friends
All the adventures that they had
And the way I shook my head
Just to pretend
That you and I weren't the main characters
Of every daydream that I penned
But we were.
We were thick as playground thieves
And friends to the bitter end.

We got older
And still found ways to rearrange
Seating charts to wind up in adjacent desks
You pushed me to succeed through all
The classes I didn't attend
Always there for each other
Explaining how teenage hearts would mend
And if I could do it all over again
Back to when we were kids
The only thing I'd change would be
To make sure you knew
You meant the world to me.

So I sat
And I wrote
Something to make you happy.

Because despite his best efforts
He could never take your laugh from you
The laugh you'd had since we were both kids
The laugh that would just burst out of you
Like your soul was built on a fault line
And I was always right there next to you
Both of us digging around the rubble
Before the search-and-rescue team could arrive.

Sext: I wanna break into your house and watch Breaking Bad on your big screen TV and you could join me if you want.

Sext: I wanna eat bagels in a bed with you.

Sext: I wanna kiss you straight through to your skeleton.

Sext: I wanna gnaw on your rib bones like I'm a lonely coyote.

Sext: I wanna kiss you right after you make some smart literary reference.

Sext: I wanna kiss you when you make a dumb literary reference.

Sext: I wanna kiss you against a laundry machine and take your shirt off and touch you all over your body.

Sext: You make me feel like an ant on the sidewalk.

Sext: I wish you were an ice cube so that you'd chill with me.

Sext: I wish you were a rotating fan so that you'd blow me occasionally.

Sext: If I sat outside your window would you promise not to call the cops or anything like that?

Bro text: I told her I thought about her when I was doing chemistry
She texted me back lol you're really not funny.

Pickup line: This is a friendly reminder that we exist simultaneously in the universe which had like a .00000000000000000000000000001% probability of ever happening so like if you wanna make out I'm cool with that.

WHEN I SAY I HOPE I DON'T SEE YOU AT LONNIE'S I
REALLY MEAN I'LL BE THERE ALL NIGHT WAITING
FOR YOU PLEASE COME AND I'LL SING YOU BLINK-182
SONGS AND OFFER TO BUY YOU A BEER.

Aysa

E,

I think this may be the last poem about you.

I should have told you
On the day you came to my house
How I felt.
How pretty you looked in your dress.

Just like looking at the sun
Makes you go blind
Looking at you made
Everyone else just a little less
Beautiful.

ONE DAY,

A day that began as any other day but will end shorter than every other day. The summation of a journey that ends with as much significance as a single molecule of water in a tsunami. A day almost naive in its simplicity of wake, rise, look for a fix. To you it will be filled with infinite meaning though to the Earth it is nothing more than a sequence of boundless motion.

YOU LOOK UP

And as your head turns it becomes the last significant action you are able to take of your own free will. There are those who say this free will is a lie. That every moment of your life set into motion consequences that would inevitably, like a Shakespearean tragedy, lead to the moment where you would look up. The eternal, unstoppable "Fuck you" from God. This is what has happened this is what will happen this is what will always happen.

AND SEE THE SUN

Which has betrayed you in your final moments and is no longer where it should be, where it was just a moment ago. The shot ricochets through the alleyway. You are no longer looking up, instead you are falling down. But you can still see the sky

ECLIPSED BY A CLOUD OF CROWS

Calling out in chorus. A kaleidoscope of black and feather. The tessellation of beating wings between the two buildings that have become your sepulchre. You were always jealous of the birds. Of the way they could float through the air with such freedom. And then your thoughts become lighter. And then you feel lighter too. And then the black of the sky becomes the black of everything. And then it is done.

Allardt, TN

The wind changed somewhere on US-127 as we passed through Allardt, TN - Population: 634 though still "Home to the Giant Pumpkins", which was how we noticed the faint smell of heated manure drifting between car windows.

Some people in the pumpkin patch waved at us and I thought how strange it must be to live in Population: 634. My high school graduating class was 634 and we all nearly killed each other at points. But here was this little town forgotten near the mountains of Tennessee where they all knew each other down to middle names and spent their lives together in the quiet comfort of backwoods country life.

In my own life I've been to at least 30 different states and been to McDonald's in 15 or 17 different countries and lived in maybe 9 different houses or apartments (mostly during the time I couldn't get my shit together). Add to that every life I've lived as a voyeur between the pages of books - in the magic past the Phantom Tollbooth or the time I've spent on the other side of the Looking Glass. And then of course there's the infinite of my dreams, where cats talk and crows caw destiny in parliaments and murders, though their wisdom is usually forgotten by the morning except in half-legible scribbled delusions. I can't help but laugh at how thin the line rests between Dream and Delirium. Then there are also countless ghosts who still breathe whispers in my ears. All of these just to get an outline of myself.

How do you remember it all? He asked me as we pulled our car into the parking lot for Subway.

See the truth is my first detention was in the first grade. I took too many napkins in my elementary school cafeteria and Mrs. Mercier made me stay in for a week and write apologies to all the lunch ladies. To this day her name sends shivers down my spine. It's not a cliché metaphor if it's true. But I wasn't alone in my struggle against the tyranny of oppression. My best friend at the time - Ruben Salzado - he was by my side both in crime and conviction and I can still see the cocky way he smiled when he told the principal's secretary "We've got detention." From that day on at least I never had to be in trouble alone.

He moved when we were both 8 years old and the last day of third grade would be the last time I'd see him in my life. But I still see his cocky smile on the faces of strangers. Sometimes I practice it in the mirror when I think no one's around me. The smile that taught me it's okay to get in trouble as long as you find the reason that it was worth it.

It's easy to remember when you think of the ways that something changed your life.

I've told the story of my first kiss before. How she tasted like raspberries. But there's a part of the story I skipped. My first kiss? I missed. I was so nervous that I closed my eyes and shoved my face at hers and our skulls collided like coconuts. We tried again after I polished the bruises off my ego, but how could I forget a first kiss like that? There was a valuable lesson that day: always make sure she knows the first kiss is coming before you give yourself a concussion.

The first time I saw Nashville I was 17 and I felt like I was as old as I could ever get. Learning to say y'all, learning that bless your heart isn't a compliment. Learning the way Natchez and Blakemore intersect and how to navigate the back roads to skip all the traffic that sucks in Nashville newbies. This was before the Gulch went from a pit in the ground to "hip". Before the casualty of Southern charm. Before Nashville's soul - its Belle Meade glamor and honky tonk dives- were swallowed by the future. By Progress.

But I remember what it was like back when there were guitar shops and thrift stores in Hillsboro instead of luxury apartments for lawyers. Back when sushi on 21st was dirt cheap, before they tore down Ken's to build one more high rise. When biscuits and gravy were a real menu item instead of a parody of a memory of what Nashville used to be.

Of course I still love my home with my whole heart. Different doesn't have to mean worse. I just remember how it used to be. And I still see its soul under its new skin. The same soul that saved my own.

In the middle of the parking lot, I took a deep breath of Tennessee Mountain air, promising myself to remember just one more thing.

You

As we watched the sun rise from my
Bedroom window it occurred to me
That I could spend entire days wearing
Nothing but your lips.

I wanted to tell you how
There were fish in this world
Desperate to grow lungs and legs
So they could walk to Nashville just to
See you smile.

I wanted to tell you that your smile
Is the most beautiful thing I've ever heard
That it echoes between the spaces
Around our faces and draws me like a
Magnet to your heart
Because it tells me everything even when you
Don't say a word.

And every time we're close I want to
Pull you tighter because even atoms feel like
Cosmos between us
When I want to kiss your neck and thighs
Then look into your eyes
To find the road map
Of whether or not this is meant to be
And I don't mean to seem cheesy
But you're so beautiful
Mountains push themselves into the sky
For a better view.

I'm looking for a better view, too
When I dig through all the pockets of my
Mind, looking for an excuse to text you
And say hey,
I thought about you today.

I hope that will be okay.

Natchez Trace

We were sitting under the overpass
Beneath the Natchez Trace Parkway
In my dream last night.
The crickets were chirping
The way they only do
On warm summer nights:
A choral cacophony.
A song in surround sound.
Those late-night choir boys
Drunk on their mating rituals
Desperate to shriek louder than the
Passing cars so that they
Might fornicate in the night.

We'd parked the car on the side of the road
And laughed (in my dream)
In the middle of the road,
An empty stretch of highway
In an empty stretch of mountains,
Then we walked down this
Secret path through trees and
Grass and stumps and roots.
You put your hand on my shoulder
Because you couldn't see without the glow
Of the street lamps and the head lights.

That made my heart beat sideways a little.

I wish you could have seen it
Seen my heart
Filled with the suggestion of matter
The way a balloon suggests air -
An expanded pressure of emptiness.
I've always been there before you
Imagining the moments and shapes of life.

But in my dream
We were sitting next to each other
Tossing rocks from underneath the overpass
As far as we could
Into a pond where sea monsters slept
And touching (not holding)
Hands.

The Lonely Bones of Winter

Love Poem

What do I know of God
Except what you taught me?
Crammed lessons of scripture
Sitting outside a café as
The sun guttered below the horizon
And the breeze tossed up the smell
Of trees in heat
All so that we could trick your father
Conning him into believing that I
Was a man of faith
Worthy of his daughter.

(I wasn't.)

What do I know of the divine
But in those moments
In which the thin trace
Of your body fluttered through my life
And the finite space you occupied
Through my existence
Seemed infinite.

In the pleasure of your skin
Pressed to mine
In the dead of night.

The taste of your lips.

The summer came
A year later, with heat heavy
From memory of the year before.
A certain perseverance and weariness
Hidden in the syllables and fringes
Of our voice.
A fox caught in a den of tigers
Praying for silent steps
And mercy.

One night
We sat alone in my apartment
And you sang the story of our love
Your notes playing out like a song
Of salvation that I almost didn't know I still needed.

You kissed me straight to my soul
A kiss that I could never quite place
The taste of
And asked for a poem
For yourself
For your birthday.
        But you said you understood why it hadn't happened.
Your songs told stories of what could be
My poems only told stories of what could have been.

There was a difference, I said.
It makes all the difference, you said.

I'm sorry that I was so late to write you this poem.
        I'm sorry that it had to be this one.

To the Ex-Girlfriend and her Next Boyfriend

1

I would like to exchange
All my previous impressions of a savior
For an impression of Lazarus
So I can resurrect myself
As someone else who does not
Still love you endlessly.

2

Do you want to know
Why my smile is crooked?

It's because I removed the piercings-
All the broken promises and broken truths
That you so carelessly embedded
Like shards of metal from an IED
And exploded into millions of pieces
Inside my aorta and my face and my veins.
And then I had to take the bleeding
Crippled pieces of your memory
And carve them from my lips.

3

The first draft of this poem
Was just me writing
Fuck
Onto a piece of paper a bunch of times.

It took a lot of drafts to get to this point.

4

Sext: When you're upset you're supposed to slow down and
count to 10.

Sext: I'm a little more than upset.

Sext: I hope your next boyfriend gets Ebola.

Sext: I want to untie your shoelaces so that maybe you'll trip
and fall down a flight of stairs.

Sext: I didn't mean that.

Sext: I miss you.

Sext: I'm sorry.

5

I want to go back to
The moment I saw you
In heels when I begged you
Not to wear heels
And I knew I would fall
Very in love with you.

6

I breathed you
Into songbirds.
I whispered you
Into starlight.
I kissed you like
You were the last
Molecules of oxygen
On the Titanic.
I dipped my hands in
The baptismal waters of
Forever.
I thought I meant something
To you.

I thought
You used to tell me that

We'd be together forever.
Now I just want to remember
The sound of your laugh
And I'm holding onto "forever"
Wondering how all that time went by
So fast.

7

I want to wrap up
The stupid pink flannel
You wore when you sang
"Our Last Night" to me
And the smile that
Lit up my universe
More than the stars ever could
Tie them up like a hobo's travel sack
And carry them with me
The rest of my days.

8

To the guy fucking my ex-girlfriend
Like two fucking days after we broke up
Or the guy like eight days later or
The one like eight days after that:

If I see you
Walking down the street
I will punch you in the throat
Until your airways stop working.
I apologize in advance.
It's nothing personal.

But when I see the two of you
Smiling together in pictures on
Facebook
(That is, before she blocked my profile)
When I see you holding the girl
I thought I was going to hold for the

Rest of my life
I want to reach through
The computer screen
And tear every facsimile of
Happiness out of your life.

9

I know it's not rational.
I know it's not your fault.
I'm really sorry that all these fibers
Of my being are devoted to hating
Someone I have never met
Face-to-face
But there is nothing logical
In walking down a dark alley
Again and again
Only to keep getting shot by the same gunwoman
Again and again
But thinking this time
Things will be different-
Just trust.

10

I still remember the way my stomach
Did somersaults the first time
I saw the ocean in her eyes
And the way it felt when
Our lips locked like velcro.

I guess that too
                    Belongs to you now.

11

I'm done
Writing you poems
And I know this one
Isn't long
But it's because
I'm trying find the
        Next page.

I hate watching movies with really compelling love stories like Silver Linings Playbook or Wristcutters: A Love Story or Spectacular Now or really any movies like that because the music swells and the characters look into each others' eyes and break down and run to each other in the middle of the street and your heart kind of aches a little bit and it makes you start to think that beautiful love stories can happen in real life. And then you roll over and realize relationships are for the birds and no one is really happy anywhere and having to share a twin bed is sweaty and uncomfortable and NOBODY has cute breath in the morning and honestly there's no such thing as "the one" no matter what anybody tells you.

It's like the first time you get high and everything is an outer space comedy show and you spend the rest of your life trying to find it again. You just keep trying to find that girl who will climb with you on top of the roof of one of the houses in the nearby development that's still under construction, the one where the two of you can sit and watch the sun set and hold hands, and you can admire her pony tail while the sun glows onto her face.

I don't think I quite have the hang of love poems yet because I've never written one about actually being in love.

AC

Right before I left the bar
The sky decided it would be a good time
To condense and come apart -
Sheets of rain and cracks of lightning
The blare of a tornado siren
Piercing the midnight stillness of Midtown Nashville.

And then the horns came from ambulances,
Parting traffic like the sea on their way to Baptist
Or Vanderbilt or wherever they were headed
Drowning out the frustrated shouts of drunk people trying
to run
Between terraces to keep from getting water
On expensive clothes.

Power lines criss-crossing above it all
Like sickly arteries humming through the storm.
The city both pulsing and hushed all at the same time

And I, oblivious to it all as I walked under streetlamps
Back to my Lexus, with doors that only open from the inside
So I had to leave the windows down
Even when it stormed.

Oblivious to it all because the only noise playing
Was the sound of your voice
Coming to a crescendo
Unlike any song I had ever heard before.

I kept thinking how I wished
You were lying next to me on my arm
Until it fell asleep, limp, stuffed with pressure,
And as the rain fell on my face
Outside the bar
In Midtown Nashville,
I decided that I wouldn't dare move it.

It's snowing.

It's not supposed to do that here. We live south of the Mason-Dixon and so there is not supposed to be cold weather here. But holy guacamole it is snowing and it is sticking to your hair as we're walking and that looks pretty as frick. The street lamps are glowing against all the little water crystals and I would kiss you a big snowy kiss on your lips if this were a movie or a romantic novel.

Interstellar

They say when you approach the speed
Of light time slows and they say when
You reach the center of a black hole time stops.

I think that might have been the perfect place to
Love you.

Inside the black hole of *Interstellar*.
Inside the pause button of reality
Inside the stopped-time memory
The center of our third date
When you brought your roommate with us
To the movies.

Your roommate who you used to make out with.

I don't know if that was weird or just a little
Awkward but I liked you so much it didn't even
Matter that you used to make out with
Anyone.
Because in a world with 7 billion people
It's true that there's gonna be a line and it was
Pretty fucking cool that I got to be your number one.

I mean, everyone has some history
A little piece of you or me that ends up
Like leftover lipstick on a cheek
And I wanted to get your lipstick on more than
Just my cheek.
I wanted you to paint scarlet footnotes to Heaven
On the Nashville chapter of my life.
I wanted to get you alone
To make the bed squeak
To make your thoughts numb
Except maybe to speak
"Oh my god. We're totally naked."

See, there's a time for poetry

And metaphors and bold testaments to romance
But when we're locking lips (or hips) there's
Something to be said for simplicity.

Like "You're really REALLY hot."
Or like that sigh you make when I know
I've done something good.

"Pffuh."

Or like how obviously your eyes were the most
Gorgeous blue I've ever seen
And even though I've said that before
To someone who wasn't you
It doesn't make it any less true.
Every moment
I was conscious I was
Consciously daydreaming myself
Towards you.

Because for a time
You were my number one.

And even though it's done
There was a time that we made
Mountains move to the scope of our infinity.

They say nothing
Can escape a black hole.
Not even light, despite
How fast it travels
Can escape the certainty of a
Tear in the universe.

Not even infinity.

Not even us.

The stars weren't out
The night you told me it had to end.

That right now it
Might be good but the
More time that passed the
Faster these diamonds
Would turn to charcoal.
The blue of your eyes fringed
With the red of your regret.

I kept hoping that
Maybe there would be a
Star to wish on.
To wish my words into
Handcuffs or space shuttles
That would keep you from
Walking out my door and
Out of my life. Except I
Don't think I'd want you
Arrested inside my life.
And I don't think you
Would like that very much either.
And besides,
There aren't any stars
Inside a black hole.

But I'm still here.
Still sitting in the center
Time paused
From the time I
Was your number one.
Still whispering into stars
That you're beautiful

No matter how slow the time gets.

Missing Out

I'm not scared to die.

When I die the world
Will not notice that it is minus one.

Somewhere, on the mass
Of land and tree
There will come another
Who will discover
The joy of dancing over ice puddles
And holding gloved hands while
Kissing with snowflakes
Swaying from the sky
Landing on her hair
Glinting in the moonlight
With the moon bright behind
Wisps of winter clouds.

I'm not scared to die.

I'm just terrified of missing out.

The Part About Ghosts

Homecoming

First, my old house. Yellow siding. A small yard.
A brick path lined with hedges right to the front door.
Leave the driveway. Go left until you reach Buttonball
Then right to Hebron. Then left again till Main
(You can cut through the police station if you know the way)
Eventually you'll reach the river.
The whole trip takes about 15 minutes on skateboard.

You'll reach the river and find a hotel that juts
Into the sky like a message to God.
Now go 10 years into the past.
Creep into the fog that spawns from
Water so clear it must be holy.
Dip your feet into the mud but
Watch for snapping turtles that sometimes
Dot the waters.

Follow the abandoned train tracks
Along the shore until you reach the highway.
Duck under the overpass (don't worry about "trespassing"
No one ever calls the cops around here)
Maybe you'll see Elle in the Wendy's on Main with her
mother.
Maybe you'll see Nick and me around Glen Lochen,
Carrying sticks as swords and pretending to fight dragons.

Maybe you'll see a crack-addled man
Twitching outside the Shell station near the colonial
cemetery
And he'll ask you for money
And you'll pretend you don't have any, hoping that
He'll just disappear if you don't make eye contact.

Open your eyes and come back to the present.
Elle is gone.
The man is gone.
I am gone.

But there is a hotel here now
So it is Progress.

KS

I just want to turn those nights into words. Those nights tucked away in parking lots with the heater blasting too hot in my face and Brand New blasting too loud on the stereo and thinking about our respective futures and how those would intertwine. Those nights where as far as I could think was the way your face and your ears and your eyes all fit together to make you look like the queen of the elves. That seemed like a hilariously funny thing to say when I was 16. I don't want to grow up any more. I want to stay in the McDonald's next to the highway and get lunch at the Subway by my work and I want to be late for curfew on the weekends. I want to hold hands on the ledges of cliffs and try to climb through massive snowbanks, falling through into the cold with every step and wondering if I get to kiss a girl as pretty as you are once the night ends. And then waking up impossibly early to go back to school and waste my days getting yelled at for not doing my homework or yelled at for not doing well at tests or getting yelled at for just generally not being as good as I could be. I want to write all the time. I just want to keep writing words down as long as I have words to write.

Halloween junior year. Was it junior year or senior year? I honestly can't even remember because they all kind of blur together. I just remember a Halloween on our friend's cul-de-sac where I was trying to figure out if you liked me or not and wondering if you wanted to kiss me on the swings of our old playground. I just wanted to hang out with you and hold your hand and call you my girlfriend and talk to you about who I was but then things got kind of weird and you stopped talking to me and kind of held back until we walked through the streets in the rain until we got to your friend's house and met her mom and dad and then I got in a car and went away with the bitter taste in my mouth that kind of said hey this didn't work out sorry kid. I know that taste really well. There isn't some kind of magic spark that lets you know that this is it and this is good and throw your life into hers and see how it works out. There's just that taste that says you goofed. Add another name to the list

and call it a day. A day swept up in so many years that it might as well be someone's else's life.
How's Connecticut doing?

Naubuc

We lived near the elementary school then
And in the autumn
When the sky was blue -
Not the baby blue of spring or
That deep soulful blue of summer
But that dull blue-gray
Like someone sucked out the saturation from the sky

We would hear the band practice -
Sounds carried on the wind:
The blare of off-key trumpets
And the pounding of off-rhythm drums
And a boy blowing air into a baritone
As big as he was.

Snow came early that year
Blanketing everything
With ice and frost
Packed tighter than concrete
And all the trees
Lost their minds
Withering and dropping leaves
Like they had suddenly become boulders
Crumbled brown leaves falling in clouds.

Nature's way -
Create beauty
Kill itself
And begin again.

Waiting for God

When God created the universe He named with words
"Let there be light" and "Let there be sea" and when Ra
Made the world He spoke "I am the sun" and
                              "This is good land"
And they took the Words and used them to shape
The Earth.

When the boy came home from school
With lips bloodied from fists swung in parking lots
He would retreat into a room lined in faded yellow
wallpaper
Broken by holes from fists swung in frustration
And gather all the words he could find.

Gather them from a lonely boy trying to find himself in
                              New York City
From a little girl who didn't want buttons for eyes
From a boy bitten by a spider who realized that
Now he had to save the world.

He took words and let them flow from between his teeth
        Teeth sore, jaw aching from earlier and from
        An awareness of what tomorrow would bring.
He took a pen and sat with a blank piece of paper
Waiting for Something to happen.

For a long time he waited.
For a long time nothing moved.
Eventually the sun
Began to set.

Every planet save this one
                  Was named for a god.

Elle
Reprinted from To Leave or Die in Nashville

Don't ask me why I was there
I'll lie
Or come up with some other reason
Why I was only visiting.
But it's true that I fell in love
In a place where the
Sheets were sterile
And where they watched me like
God watches Christian boys
When they take cold showers.

She came in on the
Third day to a chorus
Of whispers, some welcome
Some not.
But she was gorgeous
Like Mary
Only her name was Elle
And right away
You could tell
That chick was a
Train wreck
Or a train stop
That took a rain check
And wasn't going to
Whirlwind into your
Life a second time.

She had this laugh like cocaine
And a way of talking
Like a ball of string unwinding
And even under her
Red hoodie you could tell
She was too skinny
In a way that made me want
To save her.

Like a real sexy damsel
In distress.

While everyone else was
Content to whisper
I walked up to her and said,
"Hi
My name's Jeff."

She looked me up and
Looked me down and said,
"I haven't seen you here
Before and I've been here
Enough times to see everyone.

But you're cute."

And just like that
I felt like a human for the
First time since I'd died.
For the first time since
My heart had stopped beating
And I spent fifteen seconds
Proving there was no heaven
I remembered that I was a
Person who could smile
And that was the first
Miracle that Elle ever gave me.

Elle reads my poems
Though back then they're
Just mishmashes
And broken hearted ballads.
She puts her hand
On mine
But does it
Under the table
When no one's looking because
We're told pretty clearly
There's no fraternizing.

She tells me
Love's not such a bad thing
As I say in those poems. That
The sting you get can bring
Something amazing if you have
The patience to wait it out.

Back in those days I
Had a limp because my
Left leg stopped working
At the knee failing me
More by the day.
The point is I walked
So slow that I was sure
Love would be able to
Catch up to me just fine
In time.

Elle smiles in a way
The FDA should regulate.
She tells me she wants to
Be a writer if she grows up
Because there are stories
In her soul
Just begging to come out.

She tells me that
Family is just a
State of mind.
That it's too easy
To say I'll be yours
And you can be mine.
But then she tells me
We could do that anyways
If we wanted.

She tells me
You've got to put
Your best foot forward first

So you can weather
The worst together.
It's got to be together.
Then she showed me the
Picture she drew me
Of a heart with my
Name in it
Made with crayon.

I still have it
In my room
Half a decade later
Ripped and fading.
I told her hearts were
Important because in
The end we all have to
Wear our wounds in our
Chests
Like medals on our uniforms
And she said
Not to be too proud of
All the casualties
And never act like a
Casualty again.
You have to do your best and
No matter what you have
To try.

My left leg means I'll never
Be a prize fighter or
Marathon runner but
I'd still pick myself up and
Parade through the streets
Of Golgotha just to give her a
Day of rest. If that made
A difference.
I'd still try
Still take all the words
Inside me and some nearby
And do my best impression

Of a savior.
Even though I'm the barely scraping by
Son of a
Broken Hearted man and woman
Who couldn't tell you why
Some homeless men scream
That the end is nigh
But still waste it
On street corners
Yelling with their signs.

If it really is the end of days
Or when it does come calling
I won't care so much
About love or signs.
I'll just want to
Leave this world with
My face in a lock
Of her dirty blonde hair.

I told her, If I could I would
Write you something beautiful
Because I should because you're
Beautiful in a
Beautiful kind of way.

And she said back,
"That's sweet of you
But there's beauty
Everywhere
Like whenever
It snows someone
Has to say it's snowing
And we all jolt our heads
Towards the window
As if we've never seen the
Sky drop white.

And that's why you have to live
Truly live

Not just breathing
Seconds into weeks
Even a year sneaks
Up if you close your
Eyes too long.
You'll keep beating yourself
Up trying to find
Beauty only in
Beautiful things.

There's beauty in a
Kickball game
Behind these walls
Because we can't have
Shoelaces so
If you kick the ball
At all really
Your shoes fall and fly
And you know our gym teacher
Would rather be in a
High school anywhere
That wasn't here,
Stuck with us.
There's a funny kind of
Beauty in that, too.

So listen,
I don't want to be beautiful
In any special kind of way.
I'm just hoping that
Some piece of me gets
Shared and some piece of
Me gets remembered and
Some piece of me mattered
To someone else."

Elle
I wish that you could
Read these words.
Wish that you were still

Here instead of
Sitting six feet under the
Ground I live on.
Even though every day it
Gets harder to move
On my left leg
I swear I'd sprint
The second I saw you.
But it was true
When I told you I
Would try to do my
Very best to live.

I just wish I'd thought
To make you promise the same.

Boys

We lived our lives as idiots as teenagers
As boys-
The days when we would walk a mile out of our way
Just to spend ten measly minutes next to a crush.

Those were the days when I would leave
Before the sun had risen in the morning
And return home some time after sun set
Finding ways to fill all the hours in between.

Those were days when Malcolm Holmes
Would walk with his hand wrapped in bandage
After wrapping it around the face
Of someone who'd called him an alcoholic

Or Dj and Orion would challenge each other-
Sudden death duels for the love of some pierced
Girl with purple in her hair and legs that silenced
Us all even though none of us knew what we were looking
for
Between the tone of thighs and skirts.

But it was I who found our space between the two-by-fours,
The hole in the fence of what once was
The Jasmine Chinese restaurant
Now-abandoned and converted
Into a parking lot on Main Street,
Ignoring the signs that said NO TRESPASSING and
POLICE TAKE NOTICE, leading the charge
Into our private fort
Of asphalt lit by street lamps and the
Reflections of falling snow
As our breath filled the air like cigarette smoke.

That was the day I changed Cigarette Smoke
From a simile into literal description.
The day Dj handed me a stick
From a red pack of cigarettes.

I fumbled the lighter with fingers
Thick from cold and fear
Inhaling fumes into my mouth-
Incorrectly funneling the path to my lungs.

Air still ejected itself from my body
And I coughed until I was dizzy-
Dj handed me a water bottle to take the edge off
And I so desperate that I took a swig without looking

At liquid the color of honey
That sloshed, burning on its way
Down my throat. Burning nearly as much
As the fire from the cigarette.

The tang of vomit and whiskey
Mixed into the air as we
Laughed and rode our skateboards
Across our own private sanctuary

Basking in the glow of our adventures
And drinking deep from the grail of our
Immortality.

Trigonometry

"My mom asked me why I was failing math this quarter.
Do you know what I hate most about math class?"
      Elle said one day the first moment we were alone.

"It's that my leg always falls asleep.
That feeling
That tingling
Like someone's stabbing the insides of your feet and
Picking at all your skin
Like no one ever taught them manners.

"But that's not the part I hate the most.

"What I hate even more
Is how it feels when it's building up.
It's gonna hurt.
It's inevitable.
But do you move your leg right away and deal with it?
Get yourself back to normal faster?
Or do you wait for it to maybe go away
Like if you can somehow sit perfectly still
For as long as it takes
It will go away without hurting.

I can never decide."

      "To be honest, I thought you were gonna say
      trigonometry."

"To be honest,

That's what I ended up telling her."

Homeroom at GHS

Winter
A biting, bitter chill
Deep in the Earth,
Frozen ground, frozen heart
Dull days under the sickly floodlight
Of high school incandescent bulbs.

Connecticut days where the sunlight
Burns like an empty candle and
Ends with the brevity of a Mayfly.

At 7 every morning - just as the sun
Was peeking over the trees around campus,
Our homeroom teacher Ms. Murphy would call
Our names in order. Every time someone was
Absent she made sure the whole room knew.
Except you,
Dj.

You'd walk in with your skateboard and sit next to me-
The world chipped on your shoulder like
Every past wrong had left its own scar.
Like every morning you'd looked in the mirror and gone
"Oh,
You're still here?"
Then left to start your day- motivated more by boredom
Than anything else.

Ms. Murphy would smile at you
And mark you present
The way a sphinx smiles with its secrets
Tucked behind its lips-
Truths forgotten to time or never known in the first place.
I used to think it was because she'd given up on punishing
you.
Now that I'm older
I think it was something else entirely.

I watched your eyes
The day you found out she'd been attacked
By a student-
One she'd pushed a little too hard to succeed
When the rest of the world and even his own brain
Had convinced him he was a failure and ripped scabs of
insecurity
Off his self-esteem to the point where success was more
frightening
Than just giving up.

I watched you disappear down the hall
And the rest I only heard
From locker room rumors
About how you walked down to the office
Where Kyle awaited his fate.

How you
Hit him as many times as you could
Answering his blow with dozens of your own
In a language you both knew better than English, before
Mr. Dunbar -
Former college basketball star turned
Guardian of the wastelands,
The High School Principal,
The last bastion of Order in the hallways -
Lifted you off Kyle by your collar, because
Despite your snake bite piercings and your
Bravado you were still just a
140 pound kid with rage leaking from your heart like a
Busted fire hydrant.

That's the story we told of why
Kyle never spoke an ill-word to a teacher the rest of his
High school career,
And how Mr. Dunbar bought you an ice cream sandwich
that day
Before suspending you from school for fighting in the office.

October

And what has the October Moon
Taught you of the inevitable?
Its distant glow between street lights
Guiding you home on empty roads
With that dry New England air filtering
And freezing inside your lungs and
Burning the back of your throat
Reminding you that winter is nearly here
And the year keeps passing.

The years keep passing
Since the night I snuck out of my house-
So cold, so angry-
What do fifteen-year-old boys have
Inside that
Burns like fires in an oil field on the
Surface of the sun?

I walked to the bus station
Without a place to go except
Somewhere near your atmosphere
So I called you on the pay phone and
Prayed that you were home.
"I'm on the bus to your town if you'll
Meet me."

What has the October Moon taught
You of change?
The way it opens and shuts
Like a wink from across the cosmos.
When even a lover like the moon
Will someday leave us
As floating space debris,
Who the hell can say forever?

Just like faces that used to be lit by
The Moon

Now make eye contact through the
Tint of cell phone screens at parties
Like maybe everything cool is going on
Somewhere else.

We rode the bus an hour to the coast while
You tickled my arm with your spiderleg fingers
All because I told you I was
Arachnophobic.
But that somehow made my fear seem silly.
Like the days when night lights
Worked like cages
To keep monsters trapped in closets.
Like nothing could go
Bump in the night again.

-I want to get old with you
Even though we smoke and every day
My left leg works a little less,
I want to hold you until my joints
Crunch like the bowl of Cheerios I had
For breakfast this morning
And maybe then until we both are
Dust.

-Some day, (you said), we both will be
Dust.
But if you listen to the wind
I'll still be whispering your name.

What has the October Moon taught you
Of gravity?
How it keeps bringing us down;
Tying our orbits to consistency
Pulling tides to the shore
And melting rocks with the acid of
Time.

We sat on the shore until the sun rose-
Connecticut wind blowing to our

Coordinates like a kiss from across the
Ocean.
And I kissed you too, in the sand, in a
Way that I hoped would pass through your lips
And into your forever.
But who the hell can see forever?
So instead we ate scrambled eggs with hot sauce
In some diner by the coast before
Catching the bus back home-
Each glad we had met
Someone who could teach us that love
Isn't in the words or phrases
But rather the places in our memories
On bus rides without destinations
And that we're born into this world crying
Just so that we can learn how to smile
In the minutes of the Moonlight.

Elle, A Memory

You were like trying to remember a song
With its melody caught between your ears.
You were like driving in the rain at night
With the windows down and the heater up.
You were freckles and orange tic-tacs
And green Marlboros in a bright red hoodie.

You were the purple of a January night
When we broke into an abandoned house
And you told me about yourself
The way people only do when they're young
And not afraid to get hurt.
When you told me you'd
Know me forever.
Back when you knew my name.

I want to go back
To a December night
Holding hands in the cold.
Tripping over ice patches.
Kissing.
Snowflakes in your hair.
You told me getting older
Wasn't in your plans
And we dragged a cigarette
In the cold.

It's the colors.
It's the way the world was brighter
Around you.

My living room carpet
Where you held me after school
One day. Your arm around me
The green of the floor
The smell of your golden hair
Like apples and menthol smoke.
You told me

74

It would all be okay
Some day.
We would get away.
See new places.
Get a convertible
And pack our bags
For a different coast.
I still keep our dream alive
Even if you can't-
You can't travel any more.

The day we sat
In the gray fog and pine trees
And the red reflections of traffic lights.
When I asked if you liked
My best friend
And you answered
By grabbing my collar
And kissing me for the first time.

Elle
Will you meet me
Like you were supposed to
By the blue of the ocean
On a Cape Cod beach.
We'll roll up our pants
So our ankles don't get soaked
And jump around crabs
And get ice cream back in Brewster.

You would be mine again
Sitting by the beach
And I'd hold you so tight
No one would be able to tell our atoms apart
And once I died too,
And the universe took my atoms to make
New lives,
It would have to take one from each of us
One from you
And one from me

To put in all the colors
In the world.

Scars

There's an empty moment
As you lie on my bed
Breathing next to me.
An empty moment in between
The feeling of your chest rising
And your body pressed against me
And the curls of your hair in my face.

I want to take that moment
And place inside it a quiet whisper
Of all the words I know I won't say
Like
Show me your life
And all the moments you've survived
Show me the way you breathe in
October air
And let me taste the texture
Of your lips.

I want to hear the song
That two broken-hearted people
Make when they collide
Or at least
I'm broken.
How are you?
Do you function
Inside your frame?

I want to take that empty moment
When you run your fingers
Across the imperfections along my arm
To tell you the scars
Aren't just for show.
That there's a story
Inside every fact of my soul.
A scar from the night
Dj took a knife to the face.

A scar on my arm
Where I got cut too
And if you listen to the
Marks on my skin
Like braille they fill the moment
With the image of my friend
Falling to the ground
Bleeding from his face
As three kids
(We were all just kids)
Ran off like goblins
Into the alleyways
And how I held him,
Watched the mark that would
Fill his face for the next few years-
Or
The rest of his life
I should say.

We're busted, bleeding people
With ghosts trapped like crows
Inside our chests
And clockwork hearts
That won't pump in the empty moments.
But when I lie next to you,
Holding you in my bed
Waking up wordlessly every so often
Just to see you
I pray that this empty moment
Might rest infinite
Together.

Une Fin

Instead of rolling her window up, Elle paid her car heater overtime; a burning furnace onto cracked lips desperately trying to stave off the arctic January air. I kept looking over at her like maybe she'd get the hint that it was the middle winter outside and she was gradually turning us both into popsicles.

Either she didn't notice or she didn't care. Elle lit her cigarette, letting the smoke fill the cracks and crevices of her white Chevy Malibu. I kept breathing in the smell like an addict in recovery. Smoke. Heater. Perfume. Winter. The McDonald's we'd just bought at the drive-through. A high by proximity to her.

"We're reading the Great Gatsby in my English class right now," Elle said, reaching her head onto my arm across the gap of the front seats. She scraped the edge of her milkshake with a spoon. I moved my body closer to her.

"And what do you think?"

"I think it makes me want to go dancing. Don't you wish you could have been alive back then?"

"Not really," I said in between bites. "I like having the internet."

Elle rolled her eyes. "You're a nerd. You don't even wish it a little bit? I think it would be so fun to dress up and listen to jazz in a night club and drink fancy martinis."

"And be a beautiful little fool?"

She tried to smack me but the angle kept it from gaining any momentum. "I'm not a fool."

"It's a quote from the book."

"I haven't gotten to that part yet. Don't spoil anything."

"Besides, you don't even know any martinis."

"That's not the point. I was going to say I liked the book before you sucked all the fun out of it."

"Sorry," I said and kissed the top of her head. "Of course I'd want to live in the '20s with you."

Elle smiled and leaped up to peck me on the cheek. She was old enough to have her permit by then and picked me up illegally from school almost every day. I would sneak out during my free period at the end of the day and find her hidden somewhere in the parking lot.

I lived for those little hours between meeting up and before I had to go to work. Sometimes we'd sneak into my house, but that never worked out. My mother had a supernatural sense to detect whether or not I broke her rule and snuck someone into the house, and I was almost always punished. More often we'd kill time at the bookstore or the McDonald's by the highway.

"What are you up to tomorrow?" Elle asked.

"I have to work on a group project with Grace and then I'm free."

"Cool. I'm not doing anything tomorrow. We should go see a movie."

I kept eating my food without the use of my left arm. "Sure," I said in between bites. "I don't know how long the project will take but I'm down after."

"Cool," she said again. She ran her fingers across my neck for a moment.

"Your hand is freezing," I said. "Could you roll the window up? I want to eat my food without dying from hypothermia."

"Sorry for touching you."

"Don't be like that. It's just the middle of winter and you like to keep your car colder than a cryogenic chamber."

"My mom gets mad at me when the car smells like cigarettes. Why do you talk about Grace so much?"

"What do you mean?"

She shrugged. "You're always talking about her. I'm just curious is all."

"I don't think I talk about her that much. And it's not like I'm doing stuff with her, if that's what you're wondering."

She moved herself back into the driver's seat. "I never said you were. Just curious about it. You're always talking about her, you know?"

"I dunno. It's like, she's actually nice to me."

"What?"

"I just meant she doesn't tease me. I'm sorry. I didn't mean it like that."

"Oh."

"What's wrong?"

"Nothing." She put the car into drive. "I'm gonna drop you off now."

"Why? Don't be like this."

"It's fine. I've just got to get going. I'm not supposed to have the car right now."

"That's never stopped you before."

"Yeah."

We drove silently.

I tried to place my hand on hers.

She moved it.

Not spitefully
Or aggressively.

Just a movement out of range.

Who the hell can see forever?

February

The day we found out
Mary Ellen died
Dj and I sat
Stared at walls
Smoked a few cigarettes
Sat more
Until the night came out
Without stars
And we moved to his back porch.

February snow blanketed the earth
And chilled us straight to our skeletons.
The Greeks had this story
About Persephone
Who was kidnapped
And trapped
In the Underworld by Hades.
Without her beauty
The whole world went
Cold and dead.
It was only upon her escape
That the Spring finally came.
I thought maybe I
Could go find you again
Wherever you were
And bring you back into the world.

The air kept sucking itself
Out of my lungs the way
Cowboys sucked snake venom
From fatal wounds
In old Westerns.
Every pulse forward
Two pulses out.
Pulse.
Pulse.
Pulse.

I kept trying to pretend
There wasn't anything but
The purple of the sky.
And cars kept passing by
Their headlights casting shadows
Of molding lawn chairs on the snow.
Cars with people who
Didn't even know they should be crying.

Purple sky.
The moon came out
And brought the stars with it
Dotting the universe with little cosmic freckles.

Freckles.
You had the cutest freckles
When you'd scrunch your nose
If you thought something was gross
Or if I said something dumb.

I'm never gonna see her
Again, Dj.
Why did she do that?
I'm never gonna see her face
I'm never gonna hear her sing
She's gone.
Elle is gone.

I'm sorry, man.
I don't know what to say.

I'm so sorry.

Pulse.

Pulse.

Pulse.

Time passed.

Monday

Tuesday

Saturday

Saturday

Days like stray dogs

March

April

May

June

A struggle for narrative

Dear Elle,

It's your birthday today. I thought about putting flowers on your grave. It seemed like the thing to do. I can practically see you rolling your eyes and telling me, "What's the point of telling someone you *almost* got them a gift?" in that voice you used when you said true things. Well, I did get you a gift. I've been writing this book for years now. My publisher wanted it finished and in stores a long time ago. I've been scared to finish this book and finish our story and I've been selfish because I don't want this to end because I already know that it ends without you.

I love you, Elle. I love you with all my heart and all the way to the moon and back just like I said I did back when we were both 15 and sitting in the middle of the community they tried to build out past House Street. You had your hair tied back in a short little pony tail because you knew I liked it and the sun was setting right through the construction and it gave you a glow through your whole body like the whole solar system had lined up just to make you look a little more beautiful in that moment.

We sat there with our feet dangling off the edge, talking about life and the future until finally I put my hand on your hand and suddenly we were talking with everything but our words. And then you put your head on my chest and I was so nervous because maybe I smelled bad or maybe you thought I was gross or maybe you didn't like me as much as I liked you or maybe -

"I love you."

And all the noise clears out.

I biked six miles to see you that day because your tongue was a drug and I'm still going through withdrawal.

It kind of weirds me out that your tongue, the one you used to use to kiss and sing and talk, is probably all rotted away now.

I miss you. Like I thought we really were going to be the real deal and every time something happens in my life I just wish you were still around to see it. We would have graduated. Maybe you could have come to hear my speech. It was one of the very pretentious "We are the future" graduation speeches. You would've hated it. You would have called it garbage. You didn't believe in the future.

That's my regret. The haunting coda is that I go back to you too much in the past and you can never come with me into the future. You never get older than 16 and lately I've been struggling to let myself do the same. I can never go back to Keeney Cove and sit on the bridge over the water and breathe in the air around the trees and tell you that the experience of life is just so infinite and you got to see approximately 0% of it.

Do you remember the bridge I'm talking about? The one just past the corn field and past that lonely picnic bench and past the men fishing - the men who snickered when they saw the mud on the butt of your sweatpants. The bridge was always damp and covered in graffiti and you liked to smoke on it. You used to hide your cigarettes in that silver box that for some reason would smell like raisins. You'd inhale them as if they were oxygen and when we were on the bridge you used to ash them off the edge and watch the cinders float through the current and laugh as little fish scattered at their presence. But then you'd stamp out the butt of the cigarette after you'd let it burn right down to the filter, and put it into your backpack until you could throw it away into a trash can. Saving the earth one unlittered cigarette butt at a time, you used to say.

Only, you don't remember what I'm talking about. You don't remember because you're dead. Because you killed yourself.

I miss every piece of you and you're gone but also you're not. Because I still see you in memories. In polaroid snapshots and flickering movie frames. In the reflections of strangers and the corner of my eye and the little minutes of my day. You are in them all, still.

The only person I wanted to talk to when you died was you. You were my best friend and the person who helped me figure out who I was. You were the one who helped me sort out all the messes of my head and the person I will always think of when I think of my past. I needed you, and you left the world instead.

You were a bomb. You had a timer on you and there was nothing I could do about it because the same circuit that operated the timer was the one that made you who you were and was what made you who I loved.

I still tell people they can turn left on red because it reminds me of you, reminds me of the time you convinced me that the left-hand turn was legal, and it's like you're alive in the passenger seat again. And it keeps you around in my mind. I'm not mad at you for killing yourself. I'm sad for you. Because you never got to live in Cape Cod with me or drink alcohol in a bar or live on your own or eat ramen because it's all you can afford. You never got to see an iPhone 6 or listen to Frozen or write all those stories you used to tell me. You missed so much Elle, and it breaks my heart to think about it and everything you can't ever have and everything you'll never be.

There was a time when you were the most special person in the world to me and I will always remember the story of you for as long as I live. There's a place for the past, but I don't think that place is in the present.

I'm sorry Elle, but it's been a long time and I have to bury you now. I choose to live, but know that I'll always be living for you. I love you to the moon and back.

Until we meet again,

Jeff

A Poem for my 20th Birthday

1815 days as a collection of toothpicks
Under grass
And somehow you're still
So much wiser than I am.

Another cigarette.

I'm lying on a bench
By the hospital -

A different hospital
A different city
But the same concept -

Realizing that I'm still
Working my way to rock bottom.
These wonder years -

The suicidal years
The alley fight nights
The passage through the
Lives of friends and lovers
As a ghost -

In this moment we are parallel.
Horizontal on beds of wood.

Somewhere nearby
There are children playing
Hide and Seek
On their own for the first time.
You'd have told me that was beautiful
The way they snuck out
In the dying days of summer
To find the best shadows
Or giggle together behind sheds.
Probably you'd have joined them.
That was always your dream

Not to touch the sky.
You wanted to
Be the sky.
To stay out.
To go new places.
To be infinite.

You took that
When you left.
You took a lot of things.

I finish my cigarette
And let it slide
To the ground
Remembering the way
It tastes just like you did.

For Elle.
With all the love I have.

Epilogue

This is a book about a lot of things. It's a eulogy and a memoir and a book of poetry and an autobiography and a selfish piece of shit depending on your point of view. It's also a piece of my dream. A dream isn't something that happens when you fall asleep at night. A dream is something that keeps you awake at night. I think if you have a dream you have to go for it. Yes it's hard. Yes being poor sucks. But if you're going to do something and dream of something, you're going to have to dream of it all the way or it's not going to happen. You're going to have to lose things. But if you don't try with all your soul then what's the point? The blinks you have are a countdown until the blink when your eyes don't open again. Get out there. Stop waiting for life to start happening. Whatever you want to do, start doing it. Start painting, start singing opera, start dancing around in your underwear, start kissing people you love in the rain, start saving the whales, just start. Start doing what you want to do in this world. Maybe you won't be the best at it but you have to try.

Fuck you if you don't try.

Resources

Any talk of suicide should be taken seriously.

Below are resources for those seeking immediate help:

1-800-784-2433 (1-800-SUICIDE)

Texting: Text ANSWER to 839863

Spanish: 1-800-SUICIDA

Veterans: 1-800-273-8255, Veterans Press 1

www.suicide.org/suicide-hotlines.html

www.crisiscallcenter.org//crisisservices.html

1.800.656.HOPE (Sexual Assault Support hotline)

Your life matters. You are important. We are here for you.

About the Author

Jeff Ryan currently lives in Nashville, Tennessee.

There was a time in his life where that would have been hard to believe.

Acknowledgments

These are always an impossible task. My apologies to anyone forgotten in this mess.

I would like to take this space to thank my parents, as always. I know it's an old joke, but I'm amazed at how much they much smarter they've gotten since my teenage years. I'd also like to thank the people who contributed either directly or indirectly to this book through their encouragement, support, or motivation: James Kinney, Sarah Overby, Jacelyn Szkrybalo, Traci Baumann, Kateřina Zídková, Chris Rizzo, Haley Sullivan, Brandon Mason, Brett Batsel, Nick Salazar, Randy Tarkington, Dean Roger Moore, Robbie Spivey, Vanderbilt University, and the countless other people who have touched my life and without whom I would be nothing.